Murmurs of the Galapagos

Murmurs of the Galapagos

– A CELEBRATION OF THE ISLANDS IN VERSE –

Shelby Lewis Jones

ISBN: 0692968490
ISBN 13: 9780692968499

Dedicated to my parents Helen Maddox Lewis and Robert Edward Lewis Jr. (Ed) and my brother Robert E. Lewis III who by example taught me to revere and adore all living things.

Shelby Lewis Jones

*With more thanks than I could voice
to my Galapagos naturalist guide Mario
Dominguez, a native son of the Galapagos
whose kindness and professionalism
I will never forget.*

Shelby Lewis Jones

Table of Contents

Galapagos Gifts· ·1

Sea Lion Serenade· ·3

A Morning on North Seymour· · · · · · · · · · · · · · · · · ·5

Marine Iguana at the Landing · · · · · · · · · · · · · · · · · ·7

The Second Path on Santa Cruz · · · · · · · · · · · · · · · ·9

El Manzanillo · 13

Divine Bay Observations · 15

A Santa Fe Swim · 17

Preface to "Sally Lightfoot Crab" Poem · · · · · · · · · · · 18
Sally Lightfoot Crab· 19

Murmurs of the Galapagos · · · · · · · · · · · · · · · · · · · 21

About the Author ·23

All photographs in Murmurs of the Galapagos taken by Shelby Lewis Jones

Galapagos Gifts

Standing at the shoreline
Wondering if this is real?
Creatures so fearless, undefiled;
Not caring if I advance or retreat,
Frolickiing in the island heat.

Watching from a distant rock
I will give these inhabitantants
Of paradise
Their space.

Their place in time
Reserved
Forever.

Shelby Lewis Jones

Sea Lion Serenade

Sunning on the lava rocks,
Your afternoon underway.
First a nap, then a swim
And on the sand to play!

Sometimes you lounge upon a pier
Or on a harbor boat,
In command of the islands
Your yelp is really a gloat.

Letting me know you rule
All that I can see,
This is your kingdom,
A hallowed place to be.

Shelby Lewis Jones

A Morning on North Seymour

Pelicans dive for a prize
Out on the morning tide.
Sharks hover in the shallows
Waiting to give birth.

Standing on this rocky shore,
My eyes, my ears, my soul
Drink in all my heart can hold.

Captivated by the essence of this isle,
I will linger for a while.

Shelby Lewis Jones

Marine Iguana at the Landing

Very still and unafraid,
I found you resting in the shade.
Coming close for clearer sight
You didn't move (I thought you might.)

Enjoying your company
I lingered for a time
Treasuring this moment
So rare and sublime.

Only you and me
Both dwellers of earth
A brief interlude
Priceless in worth.

I will remember you in
Years to come.
Will you recall me when
Your day is done?

Shelby Lewis Jones

The Second Path on Santa Cruz

I found another path
That leads down to the sea:
A secret path that called to me.

Walking through mangroves
Sheltered from the sun,
Along a boardwalk
Built over a run.

In this secluded place
I took my time,
No need to race.

The coolness of the shade
Refreshed the journey
I had made

Vines draped around trees
As birds darted through
This lush verdant forest
I had wandered to.

Delighting in each step
I wanted to stay
But kept going forward,
Moving away.

Now I recall that tangle
Of green and hope
Someday I may return,
If only in a dream.

Shelby Lewis Jones

El Manzanillo

Up in the highlands
A giant land tortoise basks
In the afternoon sun,
Her copious lunch of grasses
Finally done.

Still alert and active
At a ripe old age
She looks wise and gentle
Like an ancient sage.

Moving forward she fends off
Amorous male advances,
Not even giving them
Backward glances!

She and her kind
Enjoy a peaceful life
That many would choose
Up in the highlands of Santa Cruz.

Shelby Lewis Jones

Divine Bay Observations

Beneath the turquoise waters
The sea turtle glides,
It's pearly shell gleaming
Jewel-like in the sun.

Bobbing up to gulp
Content and free to roam,
Steering gently through the blue
Knowing this is home.

Shelby Lewis Jones

A Santa Fe Swim

A cool dip in the turquoise sea
Banished the heat of the rocky beach.
Yachts cruised peacefully
Far out beyond my reach.

Spashing gleefully with
Small fish all around,
In the calmness of the cove
Where marine life abounds.

I smile and float face up
Studying the sky,
Owning these moments,
Spirits soaring high.

Far from home but feeling loved
By earth, water and sand:
A case of island fever,
In a tranquil land.

Shelby Lewis Jones

Preface to "Sally Lightfoot Crab" Poem

Almost as soon as I arrived in the Galapagos Islands, there was a Sally Lightfoot crab, scientifically known as Grapsus grapsus crawling over the lava rocks that line the shores. Its vivid orange body and legs make it stand out against the black lava.

Unfortunately, I was unable to take a photograph as each time I saw one, I was either climbing in or out of a boat. These easy to spot crustaceans have long inhabited the Galapagos and were noted by Charles Darwin during his research on his famous voyage to the Galapagos Islands.

Shelby Lewis Jones

Sally Lightfoot Crab

Your bright orange legs
Scurrying over the lava rocks:
A vivid contrast to the black,
You made me stop in my tracks!

A protected species
Forbidden to eat,
Intriguing to to watch,
Crawling in the heat.

Energy abounds as you
Cover lots of ground.
A Galapagos resident of long standing are you,
Adding vivid color to the landscape too!

Shelby Lewis Jones

Murmurs of the Galapagos

I have learned where Eden lies
Under remote equatorial skies:
Cloudless skies that oversee
A sacred haven under azure canopy.

Still and serene, the islands stand
Sheltered by sea, now protected by man.
They beconed to me,
I longed to go, eager to see.

Almost vanquished by pirates and greed,
Somehow surviving thoughtless deeds.
The Galapagos remain harbors of calm,
Offering themselves as a soothing balm

This unique place upon the earth
With highlands, craters and sunlit surf
Unfolds slowly to the unknowing eye
Yielding days of joy before "goodbye"

Standing in the tranquil shoal,
I vow to return but even if not,
The murmur and the embrace of the Galapagos
Are forever inscribed upon my soul.

Shelby Lewis Jones

About the Author

Shelby Lewis Jones is a Florida poet and writer whose love of wildlife and travel led her to the Galapagos Islands in 2016 where she was inspired to pen Murmurs of the Galapagos.

It is Shelby's hope that this work will in at least a small way help raise awareness of the fragility of the Galapagos and the importance of doing all possible to protect the creatures there and elsewhere from the dwindling numbers that so many diverse species are facing.

shelbylewisjones@aol.com

www.ingramcontent.com/pod-product-compliance
Lightning Source LLC
Chambersburg PA
CBHW041223270326
41933CB00001B/22